Hailstorms

By Jim Mezzanotte

Science and curriculum consultant: Debra Voege, M.A., science and math curriculum resource teacher

Reading specialist: Linda Cornwell, Literacy Connections Consulting

WEEKLY READER®
PUBLISHING

Please visit our web site at **www.garethstevens.com**.
For a free color catalog describing our list of high-quality books,
call 1-800-542-2595 (USA) or 1-800-387-3178 (Canada).
Our fax: (877) 542-2596

Library of Congress Cataloging-in-Publication Data

Mezzanotte, Jim.
    Hailstorms / by Jim Mezzanotte ; science and curriculum consultant, Debra Voege.
      p. cm. — (Wild weather)
    Includes bibliographical references and index.
    ISBN-10: 1-4339-2347-5   ISBN-13: 978-1-4339-2347-0 (lib. bdg.)
    ISBN-10: 1-4339-2361-0   ISBN-13: 978-1-4339-2361-6 (soft cover)
    1. Hailstorms—Juvenile literature.   2. Hail—Juvenile literature. I. Title.
QC929.H15M493   2010
551.55'4—dc2   2009001943

This edition first published in 2010 by
Weekly Reader® Books
An Imprint of Gareth Stevens Publishing
1 Reader's Digest Road
Pleasantville, NY 10570-7000 USA

Executive Managing Editor: Lisa M. Herrington
Senior Editor: Barbara Bakowski
Creative Director: Lisa Donovan
Designer: Melissa Welch, *Studio Montage*
Photo Researcher: Diane Laska-Swanke

Photo credits: Cover, title, pp. 5, 21 © AP Images; pp. 3, 4, 9, 16, 20, 22, 24 © PhotoDisc/Extraordinary
Clouds; pp. 6, 11, 13, 21 © Weatherpix Stock Images; p. 7 Leigh Haeger/Weekly Reader; p. 8 © Jim
Reed/CORBIS; p. 10 © Adam Jones/Visuals Unlimited; p. 12 Scott M. Krall/© Gareth Stevens, Inc.;
p. 14 © Jeff J. Daly/Visuals Unlimited; p. 15 © Thomas Sztanek/Shutterstock; p. 17 © Jim Reed/Photo
Researchers, Inc.; p. 18 © Jonathan Lenz/Shutterstock; p. 19 © Gregor Kervina/Shutterstock

Printed in the United States of America

1 2 3 4 5 6 7 8 9 10 12 11 10 09

Table of Contents

Words in **boldface** are defined in the glossary.

CHAPTER **1**
Here Comes Hail!

On a warm day, dark storm clouds appear. You wait for raindrops. Something else falls from the sky. It is **hail!**

Hailstones look like white stones. They are not rocks, though. They are pieces of ice.

Hailstones look like golf balls on this golf course.

5

Thunderstorms can bring rain, lightning, and hail. Thunderstorms form in warm, **humid** weather. In the United States, these storms happen mostly in spring and summer.

Hail mostly falls in places that do not become very cold or very hot. In the United States, hail falls most often in the middle of the country. Hailstorms also happen in high mountains.

The yellow area on this map is called Hail Alley. It gets the most hail in the United States.

UNITED STATES

WYOMING

NEBRASKA

COLORADO

KANSAS

OKLAHOMA

TEXAS

N
W E
S

Hail can cause a lot of damage. Hailstones break windows and flatten **crops.** A hailstone can be as tiny as a pea or as big as a baseball!

This hailstone is bigger than a baseball!

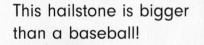

CHAPTER 2
Hailstorms in Action

Hail forms inside a thundercloud. How does a thundercloud form? First, the Sun warms air near the ground. The air is full of **water vapor.**

White, puffy clouds grow large in the sky. Soon they will turn into storm clouds.

The warm, wet air rises. High in the sky, the air cools. The water vapor cools, too. It turns into water drops. The drops join together and form a cloud.

More warm air rises, and more drops join together. They make bigger drops. When the drops become heavy, they fall from the cloud.

This storm cloud turns dark as it fills with water drops.

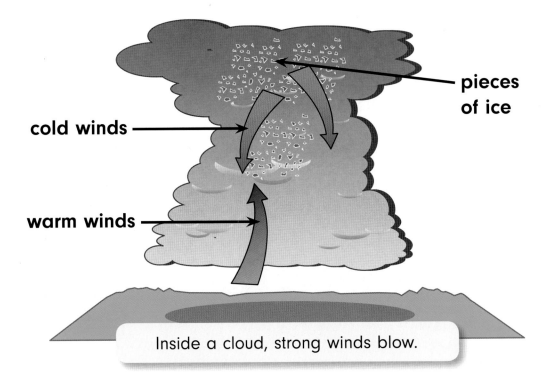

cold winds

warm winds

pieces of ice

Inside a cloud, strong winds blow.

The top of the cloud is colder than the bottom. At the top, water freezes into tiny pieces of ice. These pieces begin falling.

In the bottom of the cloud, raindrops hit the pieces of ice. The drops freeze around the ice. Hailstones form. Strong winds blow the hailstones up and down inside the cloud.

More raindrops freeze around the hailstones. They grow bigger.

Finally, the hailstones become too heavy and fall. Small hailstones may melt as they fall through the air. Larger hailstones can cover the ground.

CHAPTER 3
Huge Hailstorms

Hailstones fall to the ground very fast. They can travel faster than a car.

Hail can smash crops. It can also dent metal and break car windshields.

In a thunderstorm, heavy rain and hail may fall. The rain can cause **floods.** Hail makes flooding worse because it clogs storm drains.

Thunderstorms can bring **tornadoes,** too. A tornado is a spinning tube of wind that reaches from clouds to the ground. Hail sometimes falls just before a tornado hits.

CHAPTER 4
Hail Safety

During a storm, scientists use a tube to collect rain. Marks on the tube show how many inches of rain fell. Scientists use a ruler to measure hailstones.

What should you do when hail falls?
Some people cover up their cars and
boats. They try not to drive on the
slippery roads. The best place to stay
safe is inside your home.

These people run for cover when a hailstorm delays a race.

Glossary

crops: plants that people grow for food

floods: overflows of water from lakes, rivers, or other bodies of water onto land that is usually dry. Flooding may follow a heavy rainfall.

hail: small, round pieces of ice that fall from clouds

humid: having a lot of water vapor in the air

thunderstorms: storms that bring thunder, lightning, heavy rain, strong winds, and sometimes hail

tornadoes: spinning tubes of wind that reach down to the ground from clouds

water vapor: water in the form of a gas

For More Information

Books

Forecasting the Weather. Watching the Weather (series).
Elizabeth Miles (Heinemann, 2006)

Water and the Weather. Water All Around (series).
Rebecca Olien (Capstone Press, 2005)

Web Sites

National Weather Service Jetstream:
Thunderstorm Hazards—Hail
www.srh.weather.gov/jetstream/tstorms/hail.htm
Get the basics, plus fast facts and safety rules.

Weather Channel Kids! Weather Encyclopedia
www.theweatherchannelkids.com/weather-ed/
weather-encyclopedia/severe-thunderstorms/hail
Find weather terms at this site's glossary.

Publisher's note to educators and parents: Our editors have carefully reviewed these web sites to ensure that they are suitable for children. Many web sites change frequently, however, and we cannot guarantee that a site's future contents will continue to meet our high standards of quality and educational value. Be advised that children should be closely supervised whenever they access the Internet.

Index

About the Author

Jim Mezzanotte has written many books for children. He lives in Milwaukee, Wisconsin, with his wife and two sons. He has always been interested in weather, especially big storms.